WISDOM
and
WIT

A Little Life Book

VICKI L. DOBBS

WISDOM AND WIT
A Little Life Book

All rights reserved. No part of this publication may be reproduced, distributed, or transmitted in any form or by any means, including photocopying, recording, or other electronic or mechanical methods, without the prior written permission of the copyright holder, except in the case of brief quotations embodied in critical reviews and certain other noncommercial uses permitted by copyright law.

Copyright © 2023, Vicki L. Dobbs
Wisdom Evolution
Clovis, California
www.vickidobbs.com

ISBN: 978-1-7373404-4-7

Book Design by Transcendent Publishing

Limits of Liability and Disclaimer of Warranty: The author and publisher shall not be liable for your misuse of this material. This book is strictly for informational, educational, and inspirational purposes only and is not intended as a substitute for the medical advice of a medical professional. The deepening practices found in this book are meant for personal use and not as medical or psychological therapy.

Printed in the United States of America.

Dedicated to You...

The Reader

of This Little Book of

Wisdom and Wit.

Congratulations for gifting

yourself some time to

spend with

just You, first.

#YOUMATTER

My Gratitude Basket

I want to thank Donna Kozik for her unwavering support, fabulous templates, awesome classes, and her magical Buddha Donna moments.

Many thanks to Shanda Trofe and Transcendent Publishing for getting me across the finish line, again.

Welcome

To all of you wonder-filled folks who are mastering your *"work-a-day"* world and searching for who you are now and who you are becoming in the process...

If you are reading this on Kindle, grab yourself a special, beautiful, "you love it" journal and relax into the journey through the wisdom within these pages of Information, Inspiration, Aspirations, and Quotes. And don't forget a special pen and/or lots of colored pencils and pens to bring along for the ride. Color is FUN. If you are reading this book in print, enjoy the journal pages provided or use that special journal that is perfect for capturing your wisdom and wit.

May you find your joy in the journey and give yourself permission to live wholly as the authentic YOU that you are searching for. Live whole-heartedly!

Honor yourself by honoring this declaration...
and speak it out loud.

I promise to show up for Myself, step up as Me, and follow through with this commitment by choosing Me first and having a blast doing it!

#'I'Matter

Contents

Introduction xi

Vision 1
    Create Your Vision 4
    Quotes to Ponder… 5
    Affirmations to Inspire Your Vision 6

Inspiration 11
    Get Excited; Live Your Dream 12
    Quotes to Ponder… 13
    Affirmations to Encourage Inspiration 14

Affirmations 19
    Why Speak Your Affirmations 20
    Quotes to Ponder… 22
    Affirmations to Consider 23

Information 27
    Information and Knowledge 28
    Quotes to Ponder 30
    Affirmations to Support Knowledge 31

Procrastination 35
    Quotes to Ponder… 38
    Affirmations that Embrace Procrastination 39

Action 43
    Taking Action 44
    Quotes to Ponder… 44
    Affirmations that Encourage Action 47

Celebration 51
    Quotes to Ponder… 54
    Affirmations to Inspire Celebration 55

Prompts 59

What's Next? 69

About the Author 71

Introduction

Kudos and high-fives for gifting yourself with this "little book of wisdom and wit" designed to inspire you to think outside the box, challenge you to look beneath old layers, and encourage you to map out and track your journey along the way.

Do you find yourself sitting in your comfy chair staring out the window wondering what's next? Why am I doing all that I do and for whom?

If you've found yourself stuck in contemplation, lost in a fog of indecision, or just muddling along towards tomorrow with no specific destination in mind, then this little life-book is just for you.

In it you will find encouraging food for thought, prompts to challenge you to look through different lenses, perhaps find a new point of view, and includes mini affirmations to inspire you along the way. Think of it as a map to the treasures in your mind and the dream that lies waiting in the depths of your heart. Use it to guide you through a process of divination and discovery, uplifting, and inspiring you each step of the way.

I have been where you may be now… struggling to keep going and looking for new ways to enhance the journey. I can help you now, because I have written through and walked the path ahead and am ready to walk with and guide you down yours.

What I offer you here is a little fun and insight, encouragement, inspiration, and a pocketful of food for thought to take along for the ride.

Enjoy the journey.

Vicki

> ### *Wisdom and Wit Tip*
>
> If you use a phone calendar with notifications, set gentle reminders for you each day or several times a day… remind yourself to take a breath, pause, inhale, hold it and exhale. Remember beauty and rest in each breath.

Vision

Empower

Engage

Embrace

Endeavor

Explore

Encourage

Enhance

VISION

My vision is to **_Empower_** You to give yourself permission to put you first, at the top of your to-do list, and to prioritize your well-being and your personal and spiritual growth, first.

I believe that when you **_Engage_** your spirit, mind, heart, and soul, you unlock your full potential and unleash your Source given talents and gifts into the world.

By **_Embracing_** you first, you can tap into your authentic self, build resilience to resistance, and overcome the self-limiting beliefs you may have come to believe as your truth.

As an international best-selling author, founder of Wisdom Evolution and Head Cheerleader for the You First Revolution, I will **_Endeavor_** to inspire you to live your life intentionally by **_Exploring_** your passions, your gifts and talents, and most importantly, your dreams, **_Encouraging_** you to create a life aligned with your core values and aspirations.

By cultivating your strengths, embracing your uniqueness, and **_Enhancing_** your own personal and spiritual journey, you become a beacon of light and inspiration in the world and a role model for others.

You can unlock your greatness and gift the world with the best of you, not just what is left of you.

#YouMatter

Create Your Vision

It all begins with a dream…

Having a vision for yourself is just as vital for you as it is for me. It serves as your navigation tool to a more satisfied life. In other words, if you don't know where you're going, how will you know when you get there? You have to define your dream.

Your vision should include more than just your goals. Where do you want to be and what do you want to be doing? What are your core values? What is your mission, and most importantly, what is your sacred dream?

One key is to have mini goals (little steps) along the way so you can see yourself progressing forward into the bigger picture. Your vision is your destination, and your goals are the signposts along the path that say, "You're on your way, you're headed in the right direction, and keep on keepin' on. You got this!"

When you have a clear vision, decisions become easier, mentors and teachers show up to challenge and guide you and perhaps, even your ideal clients get in line to work with you, if that is part of the dream.

Develop your vision today. Write it out in your journal, joyfully and in living color!

VISION

Quotes to Ponder...

Believe in the power of your dreams; aim high, take action, envision a better future for yourself. Engage, get off the shelf and onto the path you lay out before you. Make your dream a reality!

–Vicki L. Dobbs

"Vision without action is merely a dream. Action without vision just passes the time. Vision with action can change the world."

–Joel A. Barker

"Dreams pass into the reality of action. From the actions, stems the dream again; and this interdependence produces the highest form of living."

–Anais Nin

"The only thing worse than being blind is having sight but no vision."

–Helen Keller

"Your vision will become clear only when you look into your own heart. Who looks outside, dreams; who looks inside, awakens."

–Carl Jung

Affirmations to Inspire Your Vision

- I acknowledge my own self-worth and my confidence is rising.

- I am a powerful creator capable of turning my dreams into reality.

- I am living into my full potential.

- I see the path ahead and know each step I take brings me closer to my destination.

- I am worthy of abundance in my life. Physically, mentally, emotionally, and spiritually my life is full.

- I am aligned with my path and my purpose. All challenges will be met with gratitude for their teaching.

- My vision serves as my guiding light, my beacon of inspiration.

With these affirmations, I will be confident. I will persevere and I will believe, reminding myself that I am capable and worthy of my dream.

VISION

Everything in this little book of wisdom is for you to ponder…

Use your journal and develop your own personal affirmations of inspiration and encouragement.

Write or draw or paint and color them. Put them where you will see them as daily reminders of your dream.

VISION

Wisdom and Wit Tip

Remember that a clear vision is your best compass, guiding you, your actions, and your decisions into the future you desire. Let your vision be a powerful catalyst for manifesting your dream into reality.

Inspiration

Be Inspired; Live Your Dream

Just like other items in this Life Book of Wisdom and Wit, Inspiration can be accessed and developed like any other good habit.

Do you find waking up early naturally inspires you? Could you use that cushion of time to think, to dream, perhaps over a morning drink or a walk in the neighborhood before your busy schedule kicks in?

At times inspiration can be lost amidst our daily distractions like pinging Facebook messages and pop-up text alerts. It's a good reason to take a tech break at times. See if more inspiring thoughts or feelings appear in that 'silence' than they do in all your busy times.

When was the last time you took an actual break? Burnout is a thing, really. Take stock of your busy-ness and notice if short or long breaks can help feed your daily thoughts.

Your Inspiration is needed in our world--take care of it!

Embrace the boundless energy that flows through your soul when you feel, better yet, when you know that the Universe is conspiring to support you every step of the way.

Your inspiration is like a tiny spark within you that guides you toward the dream. Fan the flame of your inspiration and trust that your dreams are not mere fantasies but true reflections of the journey you are on. Nurture it to its fullest potential.

INSPIRATION

Quotes to Ponder...

"Your imagination is your only limit, don't fence it in. Turn it loose. Let it be wild and free. Run with it all the way to the finish line."

–Vicki L. Dobbs

"The only person you are destined to become is the person you decide to be."

–Ralph Waldo Emerson

"Believe you can, and you are halfway there."

–Theodore Roosevelt.

"You are never too old to set another goal or to dream a new dream."

–C.S. Lewis

"You have within you right now, everything you need to deal with whatever the world throws at you."

–Brian Tracy

"By naming your act of power (*your dream*), you create force. Follow your innermost passions in life. Empower your will and your strength of force by manifesting your secret dreams."

–Lynn V. Andrews

Affirmations to Encourage Inspiration

- I am open to receiving divine inspiration and trust in the ideas and insights that come to me.

- What I imagine is real!

- I rise above fearful thoughts.

- Today is a phenomenal day and I am doing exactly what I am supposed to be doing exactly where I am supposed to be.

- Aligned with my highest purpose, my actions are divinely guided by inspired ideas and intuition.

- My creativity flows effortlessly. I am a source of boundless inspiration.

- Every day I have an opportunity to discover new sources of inspiration to fuel my heart's desires.

- I embrace the beauty and wonder of the world around me allowing it to spark inspiration in every aspect of my life.

INSPIRATION

Practice intentional awareness and pay attention to the inspiration that calls your heart.

That is where the magic is.

Challenge yourself to journal your daily inspiration from whatever source it flows.

Draw your inspiration, paint it, make a basket to hold it, write your way around and through it…

Journal your inspirational journey.

WISDOM AND WIT

INSPIRATION

Wisdom and Wit Tip

Take an adventure – do something you have never done before… find the perfect rock and paint it, leave it somewhere you know it will be found and "make someone's day."

Affirmations

Why Speak Your Affirmations

Words have power – and there is great power in your words. What you tell yourself is just as important as what you say to others. You are using the power of your words, every day, in your conversations, your writing, and especially in your self-talk.

An affirmation is a positive statement or phrase that you tell yourself, repeatedly, with the intention of creating a more positive mindset, enhancing your "good vibes" and reinforcing behaviors that serve your highest and best good.

Think of your affirmative language as one of the biggest assets in your self-care go-to bag. It can be one of the best tools you use for overcoming those negative thought forms or limiting beliefs you may have inherited or learned through life. Your affirmations are a great ally for cultivating an optimistic mindset.

The idea behind the consistent use of positive affirmation is that by consistently repeating these practical and beneficent statements, you are reprogramming your subconscious mind to create a more optimistic and empowering belief system.

It is always wise to "go positive" when you speak to yourself and converse with others, in whatever you do, and especially in how you think. Lift yourself and others up with the power of your words.

I didn't start out as a successful Realtor early in my career. I took a lot of hits to my self-confidence and my ego got beat up a lot. It is not an easy business for a confirmed people pleaser who has mastered co-dependent habits. As I learned more and better ways to be "me" in the business of real estate, my career began to flourish. I used to repeat this affirmation to myself, out loud, driving to an appointment. *"I am worthy of abundance in my life. I know my job and I am good at it. I provide an important service to my clients, and I am worthy of their confidence in me and the services I provide. I am worthy of abundance in my life!"*

One of the best ways to juice up the positive power of your affirmations is to say them out loud. Not just once, but two, three, even ten times! These are phrases you want to repeat, to yourself, in the present tense.

Speak aloud your dream; the desired state or positive attribute, characteristic or trait that you wish to possess or develop. Say it as though you already have it, or you have already achieved it. Then... Believe it!

Your affirmations will become a valuable tool for shifting your mindset, increasing your self-awareness, and supporting your personal and spiritual growth.

You can change your life, create (or recreate) your world, and write your story authentically when you use the power of your words, intentionally.

WISDOM AND WIT

Quotes to Ponder...

"The power of your words can propel you beyond your own self-limitations, speak them honestly."

–Vicki L. Dobbs

"Words are, in my not-so-humble opinion, our most inexhaustible source of magic."

–J.K. Rowling

"Be mindful when it comes to your words. A string of some that don't mean much to you may stick with someone else for a lifetime."

–Rachel Wolchin

"Be careful with your words. Once they are said, they can be only forgiven, not forgotten."

–Unknown

"Kind words can be short and easy to speak, but their echoes are truly endless."

–Mother Teresa

"Your words, like seeds planted in an open field, will grow in the hearts and minds of those who hear them. Choose wisely."

–Wisdom Evolution

Affirmations for Consideration

- I choose my words wisely, knowing that they have the power to uplift and inspire others.

- I speak with 'positivity' to create a ripple effect of kindness and understanding.

- I speak with clarity and intention knowing that my words have the power to bring about positive change.

- I am mindful of the power of my words and strive to communicate with compassion, kindness, and respect.

- I use my words to encourage, educate, and empower those around me.

- I embrace the power of my words and speak with authenticity and honesty, creating a space for trust and open dialogue in all my interactions.

- I use my words consciously and responsibly, knowing their potential to bring about positive transformation in myself and others.

Journal your journey with these quotes and affirmations. Develop and use the power of your words. Write them out in black and white and write them out in color… write them OUT LOUD with power and grace!

WISDOM AND WIT

AFFIRMATIONS

Wisdom and Wit Tip

Embrace the practice of affirmations as a means of nurturing a supportive inner dialogue, fostering your self-confidence, and manifesting positive outcomes in your life. Remember, the way you speak to yourself matters! If you embrace that thoughts are things, then you are shaping your reality with the power of your words.

Information

Information and Knowledge

When you delve into the realm of personal development, the wisdom and power of knowledge and information serve as profound catalysts for growth, transformation, and enlightenment. You might even consider information and knowledge to be cornerstones of self-awareness, gatekeepers that unlock the doors to your personal empowerment and self-discovery.

These are sacred pathways to a divine purpose and personal growth. Empowering individuals and societies, knowledge is like the key that unlocks the gates to higher understanding, wisdom, and spiritual evolution.

The power of learning lies not only in its capacity to inform and enlighten the mind, but it also has the innate ability to inspire action and instill a sense of purpose in the individual doing the in-depth and often internal work of studying that which they desire to know more about, to transform or to heal.

When you make your decisions based on the information you have discerned for yourself, you are better armed to navigate your challenges more effectively, to transcend your limited beliefs and embrace new insights. Knowledge empowers you to make informed decisions and wiser choices.

Through your own personal research, you may gain the wisdom to shape a new reality for yourself, choosing to accept that which you know, because of your studies, to be your truth and not just the "accepted" truth you have been taught or heard.

When you walk out in the world with your own information held as your sacred truth, you are better armed to overcome life's challenges and manifest your spiritual potential; the path to your divine purpose and the dream that lies deep in the bottom of your heart. Information and knowledge become sacred tools that facilitate your spiritual growth, foster your divine connections, and empower personal self-realization.

Embracing the wisdom and power of knowledge and information is not merely an intellectual pursuit; it is a transformative journey that empowers you to unlock your full potential and by sharing what you learn, you uplift and inspire those around you.

Knowledge has the power to encourage the cultivation of a holistic perspective, integrating the spiritual, emotional, and intellectual dimensions of your human experience by fostering a profound sense of purpose, fulfillment, and an interconnectedness with the unlimited potential of the world around you.

Quotes to ponder...

"Education is the most powerful weapon which you can use to change the world."

—Nelson Mandala

"The only true wisdom is in knowing you know nothing."

—Socrates

"The possession of knowledge does not kill the sense of wonder and mystery. There is always more mystery."

—Anais Nin

"The more that you read, the more things you will know. The more that you learn, the more places you'll go."

—Dr. Seuss

"Wisdom is not a product of schooling but of the lifelong attempt to acquire it."

—Albert Einstein

"In learning you will teach and in teaching, you will learn."

—Phil Collins

"Answer the call that is tugging on your heartstrings. Seek to learn. Know what you discover is sacred and share it with the world."

—Wisdom Evolution

INFORMATION

Affirmations to Support Knowledge

- I allow my inner guidance to be one of my greatest teachers.

- I am a lifelong learner and am open to the knowledge and wisdom that surrounds me.

- I speak with confidence and calm assurance because I have studied my truth.

- Knowledge is my source of empowerment.

- Information is my catalyst for positive change.

- I seek to understand my feelings and emotions through the power of self-reflection and introspection, continued study and guidance.

- I embrace divine opportunities that allow me to gain new insights, wisdom, and knowledge.

There are teachers and wisdom keepers everywhere; at work, at school, in nature, down at the barn, even next door. They are all waiting to share their knowledge and information with you. All you have to do is "ask" them if they will teach you.

INFORMATION

Wisdom and Wit Tip

Are you feeling stale and foggy? Find a class at your local community college, adult school or perhaps even an art studio and excite your inner child with an opportunity to learn something that you are interested in knowing how to do or learn more about.

Procrastination

Procrastination

What's a word like "procrastination" doing in a little life-book of wisdom and wit?

I'll bet you were taught to "avoid" it. What if you think about procrastination as something that could be a benefit for you? Could you even think of it as a sacred tool?

Here is some food for thought… Procrastination might serve as a temporary relief or escape from a demanding task. It can be a brief break from stress or the pressure of a project. It might even allow you to finish another project that may be important but not pressing. Those have to get done too!

Procrastination may inadvertently lead you to the completion of something you don't even know is actually blocking the path to you finishing some other project.

Consider embracing Procrastination as a friend rather than an enemy to be avoided. You might even consider Procrastination as an ally especially when you need time for you, time to expand your creativity or those moments of mysterious incubation when ideas or messages come through. Ones you didn't even know were out there waiting for you to slow down and listen.

Don't hide from what you need to get done, but... if you are like me, that last minute push created by procrastinating, may just be the boost you need to increase your creativity and get the job done. You may even experience a surge in your productivity and innovative thinking that leads to unexpected insights and solutions. It's OK to challenge the clock!

Take a deep breath and move into the procrastination destination and ask what you are missing, what you need to do first, before, instead of... use Procrastination as motivation and inspiration.

It's time to rethink the sacred tool of procrastination!

Quotes to Ponder...

"Sometimes the best thing you can do is procrastinate. When you procrastinate, you allow time for ideas to percolate and for connections to form in your mind."

–Austin Kleon

"The soul of genius can procrastinate."

–Oscar Wilde

"Procrastination is not the problem. It is the solution. It is the universe's way of saying stop, slow down, you move too fast."

–Ellen DeGeneres

"Procrastination is like a superhero's power: it turns waiting into a skill."

–Unknown

Never view your intentional procrastination as a fault, it may just be you taking care of you, and that is just as important as the looming deadline."

–Wisdom Evolution

Don't let procrastination become the grave in which an opportunity is buried, rather let it be the final push to the finish line, to your dream realized.

Affirmations that Embrace Procrastination

- Everything always works out for me in perfect timing.

- I have all the time I need, in this moment, right now. The calendar is not the dictator in my life.

- I focus on the present moment. It is all I need to do.

- I am in control of my time and make efficient use of it.

- Focused on the present moment, I take meaningful steps forward.

- I embrace discipline and prioritize myself as well as my responsibilities.

- I have the determination and perseverance to complete my tasks in perfect timing.

Journal your journey with procrastination – the good, the bad, and the ugly with the beautiful. Remember our challenges are often our greatest teachers as well as our sacred tools.

PROCRASTINATION

Wisdom and Wit Tip

Dance with Procrastination -

The power of procrastination when held as a friend, not an enemy, acts as a time of percolation and allows ideas and concepts to brew as you reflect in this creative incubator.

Action

Taking Action

You can plan, think, feel, and dream all you want, but it's *your* action that makes things happen.

Believe this! Buried within you lies an incredible force waiting to be awakened. It is the power you possess to act. In the realm of goals, dreams and aspirations, the gap between what could be (your contemplation) and taking action, can often feel insurmountable. You may find yourself stuck in a cycle of uncertainty, tentative little acts, apprehension, and the big one, self-doubt.

When you harness this power to act and embrace the unknown, you will unlock the door to a world of boundless opportunity, endless possibilities, and transformative growth.

Action will often lead to change, an inevitable companion on your path of purpose. While most of us don't care much for change, it is the one sure way to unearth your true potential.

Here's some good news - even small actions add up. They let the Universe know you're ready for more, that your door is open, and you are ready to co-create your vision, your dream, your best life, now.

Ponder these questions… What motivates you to take action? Do you think about how good you'll feel when you reach your end goal? Are you motivated by rewards?

ACTION

How about this ... you jumped in and it didn't work? Don't be afraid to do it again. Sometimes it takes changing directions to find yourself on the right path. Begin with another action and you'll get there!

Recognize that taking action is the catalyst for change and allow yourself to be pulled forward through change, into the magnetic force of transformation as you manifest your dreams, one step at a time.

And remember to journal your journey.

WISDOM AND WIT

Quotes to Ponder...

"Do you want to know who you are? Don't ask. Act! Action will delineate and define you."

–Thomas Jefferson

"God provides the wind but man must raise the sails."

–St. Augustine

"Inaction breeds doubt and fear. Action breeds confidence and courage… do not sit home and think about it. Go out and get busy."

–Dale Carnegie

"Action may not always bring happiness, but there is no happiness without action."

–Benjamin Disraeli

"You don't have to be great to start, but you have to start to be great."

–Zig Ziglar

"You can't manifest a dream standing still. Don't wait for the perfect moment to find you, take action now and make that moment perfectly yours."

–Wisdom Evolution

Journal your thoughts and remember to take inspired action. Embrace the transformative power it holds and WRITE ON!

Affirmations that Encourage Action

- I am a person who takes action with decisive steps towards my dream.

- I trust in my ability to take the right action at the right time.

- I plan my work and work my plan.

- I focus on what is truly essential to the journey.

- I release all fear and resistance that may hold me back from taking action.

- I am productive, and my actions align with my vision, path, and purpose.

- Each action I take is a powerful declaration of my commitment to creating the life I desire.

Take action towards your dream today and journal the journey all the way. The finish line is just around the next corner, over the next hill, and beyond that beautiful stream you are fording. Keep moving forward…

You will never find your future in the past.

WISDOM AND WIT

ACTION

Wisdom and Wit Tip

Take inspired action and embrace the transformative power it holds for and with you as you move on…

Celebration

Celebration

There are many of reasons to celebrate - sporting victories, birthdays, weddings, babies or new jobs. And there are many ways to celebrate -- parties, presents, balloons and banners. You might even take a rowdy vacation or find a quiet retreat. These are all great ways to celebrate You.

But in your "Life's Little Wisdom Journal," you want to think of celebration as a way to reinforce your steps toward success, the action you take as you wander down the path to your dream.

Simply put, you want to celebrate - on purpose.

It helps you recognize what's working well and why. Take note if there's something you can take from the moment that will inspire you further, then apply it to the rest of your journey.

Celebrating your small victories, those baby steps that lead to giant leaps, helps in building your resilience as well. When the inevitable obstacle rears its ugly face, armed with your victories celebrated, you persevere through the challenge knowing another party in just around the corner.

When you honor each small step, you are training your mind to focus on each positive accomplishment leading to a more optimistic and resilient mindset.

Party on, but don't forget to look for reasons to celebrate the success of others as well. It lifts everyone's vibe and says "we are grateful and we want more of this, please!"

CELEBRATE ON PURPOSE -- focus on the things you want to remember. When you celebrate those, you are thanking the Universe for its assistance, and you are ready for more!

WISDOM AND WIT

Quotes to Ponder...

"When you are celebrating your life, you are shining a brighter light into the world that encourages others to shine a bit brighter themselves."

–Vicki L. Dobbs

"The more you praise and celebrate your life, the more there is in life to celebrate."

–Oprah Winfrey

"Celebrate what you've accomplished but raise the bar a little higher each time you succeed."

–Mia Hamm

"Celebrate your successes. Find some humor in your failures. Don't take yourself so seriously. Loosen up, and everyone around you will loosen up. Have fun… when all else fails, put on a costume & sing a silly song."

–Sam Walton

"Life is short, wear your party pants."

–Loretta LaRoche

Journal your reasons to celebrate and celebrate yourself. Celebrate your life. Embrace your authentic self, your uniqueness, and revel in your accomplishments, big and small. You deserve to celebrate!

CELEBRATION

Affirmations to Encourage Celebration

- My day begins and ends celebrating in gratitude and joy.

- I celebrate Me and all I have accomplished, knowing there is more to come.

- I find joy in small victories. Joy flows through me.

- I am motivated by progress, and I celebrate small achievements along the way.

- I celebrate and appreciate the milestones I reach, knowing that each one is a testament to my vision, my purpose, my dream, and the action I take to achieve it.

- I honor myself and my hard work. I know that each step I take leads to the next celebration.

- I deserve to celebrate my achievements fully. I allow myself to bask in a sense of pride and fulfillment that comes with each "party."

Journal your celebrations and don't spare the party colors… write, draw, paint, throw glitter all over everything and celebrate. You deserve it!

WISDOM AND WIT

CELEBRATION

Wisdom and Wit Tip

Start now and plan the next party, dinner out, candlelit bath or drinks with friends. How will you celebrate your next small victory, nurture your heart and mind so it will sustain you through the challenges and uncertainties that will pop up as you build momentum toward the dream that is waiting for you on the path ahead?

Prompts

Wisdom and Wit Tip

Find an outlet for creative play – write a short story about anything that pops into your head or use these prompts for inspiration.

My toe ached wearing shoes that were too small as I walked home from school…

I broke open a fortune cookie and found a hundred-dollar bill…

I woke up this morning in an old cabin, on a feather mattress, the dust, like glitter, in the rays of sunlight that shined through a hole in the blanket covering the window…

The cherry juice trickling down the side of her chin looked like blood…

My dog clawed incessantly at the side of the bed, pulling on the covers and whining…

I was just out walking my dog when I turned the corner and came upon…

The phone rang and I knew who it was but didn't want to answer…

Wisdom and Wit Tip

Grab a box of crayons or watercolors, tubes of acrylic or pastels, sharpies or colored pencils or ALL of them and find a quiet place to just be present with the blank canvas or paper. Light a candle, breathe and then just enjoy the movement of color over the empty space… draw, paint, draw in the paint, spray it with water, smear it with your fingers, play in all the colors of fun.

What's Next?

Schedule your personal

Vision Call with Vicki today!

Let's put the knowledge you found in this little *Life Book of Wisdom and Wit* to work for you –

Learn how you can go from Burnout to Bliss

and

Master the Art of Choosing

You First

Who are you now?

Who are you becoming?

Who do you long to be?

When are you going to

Step Into YOU?

Email vicki@vickidobbs.com

And let's have a chat

About the Author

As the founder of Wisdom Evolution and head cheerleader for The You First Revolution, Vicki has been helping people navigate their lives and business in a way that allows them to gift the world the best of themselves. She specializes in writing and crafting virtual and in-person courses that include some form of sacred creativity or art to anchor the teaching given into the participants physical world.

Vicki is a Spiritual Entrepreneur co-creating with the Divine in opening existential gateways through which individuals can face their challenges as opportunities, embracing them as the revered teachers that they are. Using her best-selling books, courses, working with individuals and speaking to groups, she endeavors to inspire others to create their lives intentionally. Introducing ancient wisdom techniques combined with modern modalities through experiential classes, ceremony, sacred art, and story, Vicki's goal is to see everyone live every day empowered by the voice of their own authentic truth. Go to Vicki's website and pick up your free copy of **6 Ways Your Life Can Change When You Adopt a Optimistic Attitude.**

Website: vickidobbs.com
Facebook: facebook.com/sacredwisdomteachings
Instagram: instagram.com/vickidobbs
Pinterest: pinterest.com/vickidobbs33
Email: vicki@vickidobbs.com

www.ingramcontent.com/pod-product-compliance
Lightning Source LLC
Chambersburg PA
CBHW071028080526
44587CB00015B/2537